Vancouver Calling

Since its discovery by adventurous
Spaniards and Englishmen, the West
Coast of Canada has attracted people
from many lands. Although its recorded history is brief, it is rich in
tradition, resources and natural
beauty.

This coastal vista—the entire
Lower Mainland—draws millions of
visitors yearly; many return again and
again to glimpse the beauty of the
region.

The pride of our province is the
"instant city" of Vancouver. We call
it "instant" for the city, in less than
one hundred years, rose from its
ashes like an eternal phoenix, to
become a magnificent metropolis.

Today half of British Columbia's
population live and work in Vancouver
and the surrounding areas we call the
Lower Mainland. The importance of
this region is felt throughout the
province for it is the centre of industry, and a playground for resident
and tourist alike.

Vancouver Calling serves as the
visitor's travelling companion, and it
enables the proud resident to convey
to distant friends a vivid image of the
beauty of his home beside the Pacific.

There's wine in the cup,
Vancouver,
And there's warmth in my
heart for you,
While I drink to your
health,
Your youth and your wealth
And the things that you
yet will do ...

A Toast

E. Pauline Johnson 1861-1913

vancouver calling

by ted czolowski/balynn richards

Introduction

In the stillness of the land the cathedral groves of fir, cedar and hemlock dug their gnarled roots deep into the earth, creeping to the water's edge of smooth bays and coves rippled by the foraging fish.

The verdant springs and golden autumns cast their long shadows on the earth; against the sky were patterns of ducks and geese winging their way northward for spring and southward for winter.

Early explorers charted this emerald coast, named its islands, rivers and sounds, and returned home with tales of the exciting lands of the Pacific Northwest. Its recorded history spans a flicker of time — a mere 200 years.

Where tall forests stood, farms and settlements were carved out. Cities sprang into being; modern life took root to replace the grandeur of nature. The sea and mighty rivers were confined by dykes to create and tame the land. Yet from time to time flood waters engulfed the valleys to remind inhabitants of the unpredictable forces of nature at work.

In this brief span of time through the ingenuity and industry of her people, the Lower Mainland was settled. Dominated by lofty peaks, washed by tides of the ever-present sea, this area today has become home to half of British Columbia's population.

In this book, *"Vancouver Calling,"* we introduce our reader to the beauty of life on the west coast, a way of life vastly different from our counterpart, the Atlantic shores of Canada.

Vancouver is the unifying force for the Lower Mainland, an area which not only provides industries but also natural playgrounds for all its citizens.

While nature has been somewhat tamed, this region still offers a bounty, thanks to the farsightedness of its people who fought to preserve the beauty of land and sea for future generations.

Few places in the world can offer the sight of flocks of migratory birds silhouetted against the sky above skyscrapers, eagles nesting in city parks, or schools of pilot whales arching their way under the bridge of Burrard Inlet.

We are a proud community, a community of many races, customs and religions, ever vigilant to preserve the most precious gift of all, the legacy of nature given to us in trust.

vancouver

From humble beginnings in 1886, Vancouver has grown to become the third largest city in Canada.

From infancy the city attracted the hardy, the adventurous and the visionary—a rich mixture of talents, races and religions. Those pioneers, their children and their children's children gave the city its character, its heart, its voice and its conscience. By their labour and wisdom Vancouver has become a thriving metropolis and an exciting city in which to live.

Nature supplied the theatre on which to build this city—for a backdrop, snow-crested mountains; for a stage, lowlands, waterways and islets; for floodlights, sunlight on a million windows to reflect a golden sunset; and Vancouver Island anchored in front to protect the arena against the surges of the North Pacific. She created one of the greatest show places on earth, Vancouver.

Few cities are similarly blessed. Is it any wonder Vancouver became a sparkling diamond in Canada's Crown?

Her jewelled beauty reflects the facets of living, endless varieties of sights and sound to attract millions each year from other parts of Canada, the United States, and abroad.

7

As B.C.'s major port, Vancouver stands as a beacon and gateway to the South Pacific, the Orient and the lands of Down Under.

Connected by rail, highway, waterway and air, Vancouver has become an important centre of world trade. Day and night she carries on the task of building and changing her destiny.

Vancouver is outstanding in yet another way. Her park. Few places in the world can boast a 1000-acre park in the heart of a business district; a 5-minute car ride takes visitor or resident from a busy city life to the quiet walks and remote beaches of Stanley Park.

Vancouver is the hub of a wheel. Its spokes radiate to the neighbouring municipalities, districts, towns and cities—places without visible barriers or boundaries to mark a beginning or an end. The area is known as the Lower Mainland.

Here we portray the City of Vancouver not by statistics, but by her moods, her heart and her people. She casts her spell on both resident and visitor; and many a visitor returns to become tomorrow's proud citizen.

(left) Robson Street looking east. Robson Street between Howe and Broughton Streets is known as "Robsonstrasse," a centre of European import stores, specialty shops, food stores and restaurants.

(top) Chinese New Year Parade

(top) Centennial Fountain, Court House

10

(lower) Home of R.C.M.P. schooner St. Roch beside Maritime Museum

(lower) Granville Street

(top) Royal Canadian Mounted Police

(centre) Winter silhouette

(lower) B.C. Vintage Car Club

(top) Fountain, Queen Elizabeth Theatre

11

(lower) Steel sculpture, H. R. MacMillan Planetarium

Gastown

In 1858 Captain Jack Deighton, known as Gassy Jack, came to the Colony of British Columbia to seek his fortune in the Fraser River Gold Rush. He found no gold so he became a Fraser River sternwheeler pilot.

On September 29, 1867, he set out in a canoe, with his Indian wife, her cousin, a guide, two weak-back chairs, a barrel of whiskey and a curious yellow dog; to explore the mill settlement of Hastings (3 blocks east of Gastown today).

Gassy, named for his gift of the gab, was also a visionary who saw great potential for Hastings. Why walk 15 miles to New Westminster and back when one's thirst could be quenched at his Globe Saloon set up in Maple Tree Square?

Today Gastown still manages to retain the flavour of the late 1800's. It has quaint alleys, antique and specialty shops, restaurants housed in old warehouses and its own "Mayor." Its leisurely pace delights those intent on recapturing the spirit of Vancouver's pioneer days.

A 5-minute walk will take you to the second-largest Chinese community in North America, Vancouver's Chinatown, with its exotic oriental wares, tea houses and over 30 restaurants catering to Cantonese and elaborate Mandarin cuisine.

Gateway to the Pacific, Vancouver handles millions of tons of cargo a year, including huge quantities of grain and lumber. Plans are underway to expand port facilities.

Vancouver also caters to pleasure boats, commercial fish boats, container traffic and luxury liners.

16 *The West End is one of Canada's highest density areas. In the
    early sixties it was a blend of large old homes and small apartments.
    Today 38,000 residents live in this 350-acre area within an easy
    walk of downtown Vancouver.*

There are still oases of grassy walks, sandy beaches,
tree-lined boulevards, and glorious sunsets sweeping English Bay.   17
Nearby Stanley Park invites all to explore its wilderness.

English Bay

On July 1, 1911, the sun drew the fun seekers to the beach. Bands played, people danced on the old English Bay Pier, canoes circled offshore, and children frolicked in the waves.

Dog-paddling to the rafts, they sailed down a glinty copper chute under the watchful eyes of their beloved friend, Joe Fortes. Old Black Joe was there to save them. In a large voice he'd order, "You jump off dat raff or I'll leave ya here all night." And jump they did, and swim they did!

These were the Golden Years. Well-starched little boys and girls went to parties and primly ate ice-cream shaped into peaches and pears. Dignified matrons held their "at home" visiting days each month. Young people strummed banjos from hammocks laced to soft maple trees. Folks rocked on spacious verandas hidden behind hedges and box trees trimmed to glorious shapes. Delivery boys whistled their way up back lanes to mansions decked with turrets and gingerbread-work. Street cars ran down the middle of main streets, while bicycles and trotters tried to keep out of the way of the newfangled automobiles.

Yes, these were the Golden Years at English Bay!

(top) Alexandra Park Bandstand, erected 1911

(lower) Catamarans line up for day's sail

op left) Fountain Memorial to Joe Fortes
Alexandra Park

(top middle) Annual New Year's
Polar Bear Swim (begun in 1922)

Tugboat plying waters of English Bay

(top) Easy, boys!

(lower) That water's cold!

(top) *Time out for a rest*

(top) *The sandcastle set*

(lower) *Sunset view of anchored ships in English Bay*

Stanley Park

The park was there, a 1000-acre peninsula jutting into Burrard Inlet —the habitat of deer, cougar, bear and muskrat; a woodland blanketed with Douglas fir, cedar and hemlock; a dense forest where light filtered among swaths of shadows over narrow Indian trails—where moss hung in velvety clusters—where silence was made sweet with the song of birds and the wild fragrance of flowers. A tract of land with lakes and streams where duck and geese nested and the beaver built his dam; a beckoning ground fringed by waves scooping out coves and sand crescents; a place where Indian settlements stood on grassy swards; a launching place for their canoes at the sea's edge; a region surrounded on three sides by an inlet yielding salmon, cod, herring and crab.

This verdure stood for centuries —before the coming of the Indian, before the coming of the white man. Its green tapestry was destined to belong to the City of Vancouver.

On October 29, 1889, His Excellency Lord Stanley of Preston, G.C.B., Governor-General of Canada, dedicated the park: "To the use and enjoyment of peoples of all colours, creeds and customs, for all time, I name thee Stanley Park."

Stanley Park is known the world over as one of the finest of natural parks, a place to get away from it all.

A 5-minute drive from downtown Vancouver takes you into the park where you can follow the 7-mile perimeter, catching sight of rockeries and flower gardens, beaches and picnic areas, playgrounds and swimming pools, historic sights and lookout

points displaying the splendor of this region.

As you stroll into its heart you discover Beaver Lake adorned with lily pads, a stream inhabited by ducks and swans, silent trails, a meadow laced with willows—all the beauty that brings tranquility to the soul.

The park is a fun place, too! There's a miniature train waiting at Stanley Park Junction, big enough for adults, ponies to delight the children, a zoo where polar bears frolic all year round and the Vancouver Public Aquarium, Canada's finest.

Nearby is a dining pavilion where you can have afternoon tea; in Malkin Bowl open-air concerts and muscials make their appearance during summer.

For exercise take to the tennis courts, an 18-hole pitch and putt course, grass hockey and cricket pitches, or boat on Lost Lagoon as Indian poetess Pauline Johnson did when she lived in the West End.

In Stanley Park you can do your own thing—participate in a bevy of sports, sight-see with friends or visitors, or seek out places where you can be alone.

The Park belongs to you. It is yours to enjoy!

DANG
THESE ANI

(right) At Vancouver's Public Aquarium, Skana, the killer whale, happily performs for visitors in her new 480,000-gallon pool, along with playmate Hyak, and dolphins Diana, Thetis and Apollo.

(top) Stanley Park Zoo and Vancouver Public Aquarium

28

(lower) The Nine O'Clock Gun

(lower) Figurehead, Empress of Japan

(top) Languid Ceperley Meadows

(lower) Youthful reflections

(top) Swans on Lost Lagoon

31

(lower) Beaver Lake family

Once upon a time, according to an Indian legend, the young Squamish chief, Slay-kay-ulsh, waded into the sea to purify himself before the birth of his child. The Gods ordered him out of the water. When he refused, they turned him into stone —*Siwash Rock (left)*.

Like an eternal guardian washed by the tides, it stands to greet or wave goodbye to visiting ships.

Nearby in a shadowy glen at Ferguson Point is the Memorial to Indian poetess, E. Pauline Johnson, 1861-1913, Tekahionwake.

Stanley Park's seawall which passes by Siwash Rock has a history of its own.

Begun in 1914, its creation is largely due to James Cunningham, a master stonemason employed by the Parks Board, who devoted his life to building the wall, stone by stone. Cunningham died in 1963 before the last section was completed. A plaque commemorating his 32 years of dedication is embedded in a cliff near Siwash Rock.

This picturesque pathway, eventually to girdle the park, reflects her ever-changing mood.

Stanley Park offers something for everyone. For the weary, solitude; for the harassed, a resting spot; for the venturesome, hidden trails; for all, a never-ending experience with nature.

Prospect Point (bottom left).

Kitsilano/Point Grey

Kitsilano Beach is named in honour of the Indian Chief Khahtsahlano who built his home at Chaythoose (Prospect Point) in Stanley Park.

The residential district of Kitsilano is active in community affairs. During summer the Kitsilano Showboat features a range of talents at its outdoor theatre on the beach.

Off Burrard Street Bridge, at Vanier Park, is a cluster of scientific, historical attractions. Here are situated the Vancouver City Archives with historical records of events, the H. R. MacMillan Planetarium, and Centennial Museum displaying artifacts of Indians and settlers, the Maritime Centennial Museum, and the R.C.M.P. schooner St. Roch, the first ship to navigate the Northwest Passage both ways.

On Kitsilano district's westerly edge is Point Grey's Pioneer Park where you'll find the early history of Vancouver in the Old Hastings Mill Store Museum, run by the Native Daughters of B.C., Post No. 1.

Point Grey, a hillside community of lovely homes, overlooks the beaches of Jericho, Locarno and Spanish Banks. A family pastime, in season, is catching smelts with everyone helping to net these tiny, delicious fish. These beaches are patrolled with areas of grass and trees for picnickers and nearby concession stands for those in a hurry.

(top) Kitsilano Beach looking towards West End highrises

(lower) What's new?   *(lower) Engine No. 374 (1887)–perennial favourite of small fry*

Looking northwest from Spanish Banks

(top) *Awaiting a smelt run*

(lower) *Doing your own thing*

Helping hands

37

Nitobe Memorial Garden

Along Marine Drive at the north-western edge of U.B.C.'s campus is Nitobe Memorial Garden, so named for the late Dr. Inazo Nitobe, world-famous for his work in international peace during the 30's. The Garden, officially opened in 1960, was designed by Professor K. Mori who created an authentic Japanese garden.

Walk past groves of maple and flowering cherry trees, past iris beds splashed in blue, purple and white to the quaint Japanese Tea House and Tea Garden. A miniature waterfall with a base of stepping stones empties into a one-acre lake filled with golden carp and graced by five bridges.
Six Japanese lanterns stand in serene settings throughout. Shown here at the left is the famous Snow Lantern, The Yukimi, named for its beauty is thought to be greatest under a veil of snow.

Nitobe Garden, with its spectrum of colours of the seasons, is one of the many gardens of the University Botanical Garden complex and is open to the public all year long.

Totem Park contains a collection of art of the Kwakiutl and Haida Indians of the Northwest Coast.

The Haida village displays a communal dwelling and grave house, totem poles and free-standing carvings, while the Kwakiutl village includes an outline of a dwelling house with several family crest carvings.

Plans are underway to build a new Museum of Anthropology on U.B.C.'s campus. It will include the Koerner Collection of Tribal Art, which is described as one of North America's most outstanding private collections, and will contain 10,000 artifacts of Coast Indians. The new museum, commemorating the centennary of British Columbia's entry into Confederation, will be opened in the Spring of 1975 and will house the present Totem Park collection.

University of British Columbia

On the tip of Point Grey, overlooking the blue
waters of the Strait of Georgia, is the burgeoning
campus of the University of British Columbia.
Begun in 1915, U.B.C. moved to its present loca-
tion in 1925 and today contains over 300 permanent
buildings worth over 100 million dollars.

Twenty-five thousand students engage in under-
graduate and postgraduate work, with advanced
studies in Asian and Slavonic Research, Ecology
and Industrial Relations, to name a few.

It offers degrees in Agricultural Sciences,
Applied Science, Arts, Commerce and Business
Administration, Dentistry, Education, Forestry,
Graduate Studies, Law, Medicine, Pharmaceutical
Sciences, and Science.

This old-yet-new university derives an international flavour from students who come from many
parts of the globe to study.

*Queen Elizabeth Park is famous for its beautiful botanical gardens created
from barren rock quarries. Bloedel Floral Conservatory (right) displays
tropical plants from the world over, under the first-of-its-type triodetic dome (left).
The complex contains plazas, coloured fountains and the distinctive
Henry Moore sculpture, "Knife-Edge, Two Pieces" (left).*

Pacific National Exhibition plays host to over a million visitors during its
annual 17-day fair (fifth largest in North America). It is also the centre
of year-round activities featuring major trade and consumer shows, and forms
a hub for football, soccer, horse racing, skating and NHL hockey. Expanded
and modernized, today it covers 172 acres and grosses millions each year.

Looking down on Coal Harbour, the cradle of the city, we bid farewell to Vancouver and wing forth to explore her surroundings, from the lofty mountains of Garibaldi Provincial Park to the lush pastureland of the Fraser Valley.

north
vancouver

On the north shore of Burrard Inlet are the City and District of North Vancouver, which are governed separately.

Formerly a tiny sawmill settlement called "Moodyville," the City of North Vancouver is now a bustling centre of commerce and industry, with the largest shipbuilding establishment in the province.

Ships from the north shore area carry grain, sulphur, lumber and manufactured goods to various world ports.

The District of North Vancouver has expanded rapidly in its resident-ial development, for it offers its Vancouver-bound citizens a rustic setting at Vancouver's edge.

The two largest parks in the District are at Capilano Canyon and Lynn Canyon. Both are known for breathtaking walks over suspension bridges which span gorges and the rushing waters of the Capilano River and Lynn Creek. Southeast at Dollarton lies picturesque Cates Park with launching facilities and pretty picnic areas.

The largest aerial tramway in Canada, Grouse Mtn. Skyride, travels the mile journey to the summit for a spectacular view of Vancouver and environs. Here are year-round facilities, sight-seeing, hiking, and day and night skiing during the season.

The distant echoes of "Moodyville" with its haunting Indian settle-ments can still be felt in the quiet bays, dense woods and rocky gorges which slash through mountains to the inlet.

Capilano Canyon Suspension Bridge

Cleveland Dam

Residential community of the North Shore

Deep Cove

On March 5, 1970, North Vancouver's St. Stephen's Roman Catholic Church (left) provided the setting for the wedding of Canada's only prime minister to be married in office.

Despite blizzards which delayed his arrival, Pierre Elliott Trudeau (alias Pierre Mercer) managed to elude the public to provide his bride, Margaret Joan Sinclair, with a quiet wedding attended only by family members.

Lynn Valley's Twin Falls

From the snow capped summit of Mt. Seymour to the kaleidoscopic beauty of Park and Tilford Gardens, residents and visitors share the resplendency of nature.

Hiking, picnicking and skiing are outdoor pleasures to be enjoyed at Mt. Seymour, a Provincial Government Park.

Park and Tilford Gardens were dedicated as proof that an industrial site can enhance the natural beauty of surrounding areas.

Six distinct Gardens—including the Rose and Oriental—delight thousands of visitors throughout the year. In December a fairyland of lights and tropical plants greets the festive season.

"In the blood"

*"Why have they come here?
Are they trying to learn
our mighty secrets?"*

"In the blood," a stage play by Reg Watts, was first presented in North Vancouver's Centennial Theatre the week of June 19, 1971, to celebrate British Columbia's 100th Birthday.

The two-act play depicts the lives of the West Coast Indians and the pioneer settlers. It deals with the conflict between the cultures as seen through the eyes of the adults and their children.

When the white man came, the Indian way of life was uprooted and changed. But today the Indians are deeply involved in a revival of their age-old culture. Each generation passes along the ancestral wisdom, legends, rituals and art, in the music and poetry of forest, sky and sea.

Today, as in the past, the voices of their many talented people can be heard — Henry Hunt, Kwakiutl carver, authors George Clutesi and the late Dominic Charlie, Frank Calder, M.L.A. for Atlin, Len Marchand, M.P., Kamloops, Roy Hanuse, artist, actor Len George and his famous actor-father, Honorary Chief Dan George of the Squamish Tribe and Canada's goodwill ambassador—these are but a few of British Columbia Indians preserving a fascinating culture which gives us all a rich knowledge of the history of their land.

On the page opposite are four scenes and brief passages from the play, "In the blood."

"Take time to pause, consider this."

"Then you come to my school!"

"We are the people of the forest."

". . . let us celebrate by joining
these two people in marriage."

Maypole Dance

west vancouver

In 1912 West Vancouver's pioneers little realized that in a short 60-year span their newly-formed municipality would blossom into a heavily populated community.

Just a summer community in early days, it is now an elite residential area with excellent highways, modern shopping areas, cultural and recreational facilities.

The catalyst was the building of the Lions Gate Bridge, in the 30's, which spanned Burrard Inlet to link West Vancouver to the Lower Mainland. Since then West Vancouver has never looked back.

West Vancouver has a profusion of parks — 27 of them dot the landscape, hug the shoreline, or nestle in glades. The largest, *Ambleside Park, (left)* has many children's facilities.

Other beauty spots include Lighthouse Park which juts to the sea where Point Atkinson Lighthouse stands guard over ships; Whytecliff Park with its spectacular view of Howe Sound; Eagle Harbour, Fisherman's Cove and Horseshoe Bay with moorage for pleasure boats.

West Vancouver is mountain-side living with views of ridge upon ridge of mountains, snow-capped peaks and the inlet providing a blue playground for sailboats scudding before the wind.

West Vancouver — gracious living with a magnificent mountain backdrop and tidal shores.

(top left) Named one of North America's most beautiful golf courses, Capilano Golf and Country Club lies adjacent to the opulent residences of British Properties.

(top right) The first of Canada's large suburban shopping centres, Park Royal features 114 specialty shops and services, including two major department stores.

(left) Luxury apartments fringe shore of West Vancouver, offering residents a sweeping view of Vancouver and Stanley Park.

(top) Point Atkinson Lighthouse

(lower) Fisherman's Cove

(lower) B.C. Ferries at Horseshoe Bay Terminal

(right) Howe Sound from Whytecliff Park

Along mountain-backed Seaview Drive which skirts Howe Sound is *Shannon Falls, (far left)* a 1100-foot waterfall fed by the Coast Mountains. At its base amidst the roar of water, the whisper of trees, the smell of pine, is Shannon Falls Park, a 25-acre wilderness owned by Carling Breweries.

In the past two years, Carling has donated funds to the Squamish Ecological Organization to clear, expand and mark trails and tree species. The organization is working closely with the Carling Conservation Club to preserve the beauty spots of British Columbia.

North of Squamish is tree-fringed *Alice Lake (left)*—a popular spot for swimming, sailing, hiking and camping.

Nearby *Garibaldi Provincial Park, (above)* a vast 480,000-acre region, offers ice-clad peaks, alpine meadows, jewelled lakes and winding trails—truly a place of beauty!

burnaby

From 1859 to 1868 when New Westminster was the capital of the Colony of British Columbia, Burnaby was little more than a hastily cut, rough road with a few scattered farms and logging camps. The 15-mile Douglas Road was the mainland route from New Westminster to Burrard Inlet for several years.

In 1889 the Central Park Interurban Line connected Vancouver to New Westminster, and Burnaby began to develop slowly from a farming and lumbering community to an industrial area. Burnaby was incorporated as a District Municipality in 1892.

Called the bedroom community of Vancouver for years, today its corridor position between Vancouver and New Westminster makes it a principal manufacturing centre in the province. Its economy is diversified, with service industries ranking first, followed by trade, and manufacturing centered around steel, electronic equipment, forest and milk products.

For a look at history, there's Burnaby Art Centre in Century Gardens near Deer Lake. This 20-acre site contains the Burnaby Art Gallery, the James Cowan Theatre and Heritage Village, Burnaby's centennial project.

Larger parklands include: Burnaby Mountain, Robert Burnaby, Central, Deer Lake and Century Gardens. The largest, Central Park, has a swimming pool, two stadiums, numerous playing fields and 100 acres of natural forest.

Central Park

(top) Sundays on Deer Lake

(lower) Heritage Village, 1890's

Ribbons of highway bisect the Municipality of Burnaby with Burnaby Lake on the left and Deer Lake on extreme right. Right, centre is Heritage Village and Century Gardens, with Burnaby's Civic Centre below.

71

Simon Fraser University

Simon Fraser University stretches along the crest of 1200-foot high Burnaby Mountain, overlooking both mountains and inlet. Its sprawling 1200-acre site was donated by the Municipality of Burnaby. S.F.U. was dubbed an "instant" university as its first building phase was completed in less than two years.

The prize-winning design of Erickson-Massey focuses on the scheme of core buildings which form a robust spine along the ridge and from which other future buildings can spread—down the mountainside. The *Academic Quadrangle (upper right)* reminds one of the ancient Parthenon perched atop the Acropolis. The entire complex has protected walkways so you can stroll its length entirely under cover.

Since it opened in 1965, the university has graduated over 3,500 students in the Faculties of Arts, Science and Education, and offers a trimester system in spring/summer/fall. Lower mainlanders don't acknowledge winter!

Nearby at Burnaby's *Centennial Park (bottom right)* you can enjoy a picnic setting and sparkling view of Vancouver.

new westminster

Oldest city on the mainland, New Westminster received its name and title, Royal City, in 1859 when Queen Victoria personally named it as the first capital of the new Crown Colony of British Columbia.

Planned first on paper by the Royal Engineers of England, its site along a steep hill, with a sweeping view of the Fraser, was chosen with an eye to military defence!

Today it stretches from Burnaby's eastern boundary to the Fraser River to form a business and commercial hub for the Lower Fraser Valley. New Westminster has one of the finest year-round fresh water ports on North America's westcoast, with a deepsea harbour bustling with gillnetters, tugs, lumber barges and ocean-going freighters.

The city has three unusual attractions. It is the home of Canada's only Lacrosse Hall of Fame (adopted in 1870 as Canada's National Sport). Its May Day Celebrations feature the largest children's festival of its type. Its 21-gun Hyack Anvil Salute, in memory of Queen Victoria's birthday, maintains a one-hundred year-old tradition found nowhere else in Canada.

Twenty-one gun salute, Hyack Anvil Battery

May Day festivities

In 1864 William Irving, a deep-sea captain who skippered early sternwheelers in B.C., built this Victorian home for his wife, Elizabeth, and their five lively children.

Irving House, at 302 Royal Avenue in New Westminster, has now become Irving House Historical Centre, and the Royal City Museum was added to the lower terrace in 1964. This fascinating museum is full of historic treasures dating to the days of Governor Douglas in 1858, and the 14-room house has many period pieces of the gold-rush era. It is owned by the City of New Westminster and managed by the Native Sons and Daughters of B.C., Post No. 4.

New Westminster is also a city of parks and gardens. Its largest park, Queens Park, features a Children's Zoo, stadium and picnic grounds and sets the stage for the Annual May Day Festivities.

Adjacent to City Hall is the Garden of Friendship built in 1963 to mark the union of New Westminster as the first Canadian city to establish a city relationship with Moriguici, Japan. The Japanese-styled Garden has fragrant flower beds and stands of old trees. A bridge, waterfall and pool complete the oriental setting.

Industrial view looking south towards Annacis Island

Pattullo Bridge and railroad bridge span the Fraser River, connecting Surrey to the City of New Westminster.

richmond

South of Vancouver on the silt-rich Fraser Delta lies the Municipality of Richmond, occupying Sea Island and Lulu Island in the Fraser River.

On Sea Island is Richmond's main industry—the 32-million-dollar Vancouver International Airport which employs 5,000 people. Nearby are fine restaurants and modern hotels.

Richmond has many primary and secondary industries including lumber, paper products, steel processing and fishing packing.

Richmond also flourishes with lovely homes, apartments, condominiums and gardens. Close at hand are shopping facilities, an art and museum centre, parks and community centres focusing attention on soccer, track and lacrosse.

On the sprawling south and eastern areas of Lulu Island are the fertile vegetable farms for which Richmond is famous, and surrounding the municipality is a network of dykes—just the spot for a stroll and bird's-eye view of the area.

On its westerly corner is the village of *Steveston (left)* which began in the late 19th century and over the years attracted many Japanese fishermen. Today this Japanese community has its own centre with native sports and activities.

Richmond, an active community of 70,000, is one of the fastest growing areas in the Lower Mainland.

fraser valley

The Fraser begins in the majestic Rockies and courses through canyons for a thousand miles before reaching a 100-mile-long delta. In 1808 Simon Fraser navigated the river to within a few miles of its mouth.

Above Hope the Fraser funnels through Hell's Gate to spread swift waters along the fertile delta. Fickle like a woman, she changed her mind many times over the centuries, sometimes building up silt in one area, only to take away the aluvial deposit from another. Today she seems almost tamed.

The Fraser became famous in the 1850's when gold was discovered and thousands of miners rushed to seek their fortunes. When gold gave out, they stayed to reap the harvest of dairy, fruit and vegetable farms. They netted millions of salmon and gave the Fraser the title of "greatest salmon river in the world!"

The Fraser River Delta, a giant waterway, provides a freightway system for bulk carriers, cargo ships, fishing vessels, and barges, and access to the industrial plants. This region employs one-quarter of a million people, and thriving towns and cities dot the valley to Hope.

The valley spells a wonderland of sights and sounds — lofty mountains, gentle fields, hidden parks, serene lakes and playful streams — a haven for its people, a paradise for its visitors.

Delta

Delta, in the southwestern corner of B.C.'s mainland, has superb access to the Pacific, and today is one of the fastest growing communities. Delta is made up of Ladner, North Delta and South Delta (Tsawwassen). Despite its industrial growth, Delta is still greatly dependant on agriculture and commercial fishing.

For the history buff there's Delta's Historical Museum. For the sports enthusiast try harness racing, golfing, boating, swimming or clam digging, with beautiful Boundary Bay skirting the southern shores.

For the nature lover there's *G. C. Reifel Waterfowl Refuge (left)* —a bird sanctuary for all seasons, with 175 species seeking haven on a marshy estuary of Westham Island. This 850-acre refuge supports Canada's largest wintering waterfowl population.

At Tsawwassen is the *B.C. Ferry terminal.* Ferries ply between here and Victoria, with routings to B.C.'s many islands, including the scenic Gulf Islands.

South of Westham Island is the superport of *Roberts Bank (bottom, right)* which permits the loading of 200,000-ton bulk carriers.

East of Tsawwassen is the residential/resort city of White Rock, the picture-window of the Pacific!

Surrey

Surrey, B.C.'s largest municipality, takes in the townships of Cloverdale, Whalley, Newton, Guildford and Sunnyside.

In addition to its many shopping centres, Surrey is a land of country living with streams filled with trout and flounder, roadside stands heaped with fresh produce and river beaches hiding succulent clams.

In 1882 twin brothers David and Peter Redwood each inherited a 40-acre homestead from which they created a botanical wilderness. After their third house was destroyed by fire, they built a *tree dwelling (top, left)* which served as their home for several years. After their deaths this forest area became a municipal park, "Redwood Park."

This beautiful 65-acre woodland is filled with over a hundred varieties of trees from all over the world, and is located 2 miles north of the Canadian border.

Helping to preserve the pioneer heritage of our province is Surrey Centennial Museum housing a large artifact collection.

The old west comes alive every Victoria Day holiday when the Annual Cloverdale Rodeo lures cowboys from all over North America to compete in bareback riding, calf roping and chuckwagon races—real crowd thrillers, with many a cowpoke hitting the dust!

Fort Langley

In 1827 the Hudson's Bay Company built a fort at Derby on the Fraser River as an important trade link with the Indians and traders. In 1839 a new fort was built two miles farther up the Fraser where it prospered as a fur trading post, a fishery, a farm and a manufacturing centre.

The Fort, with imposing 18-foot high palisades and bastions, stood on a plateau overlooking the lush meadowlands of the somnolent Fraser Valley. Inside were 15 wooden buildings including the Big House and the residences of the trader, cooper, blacksmith and boatbuilder.

During the 1858 Gold Rush, Fort Langley supplied eager miners with provisions and served also as an export depot for pelts, salmon, fresh produce and barrel staves. At night the Fort rocked with activities as settlers danced and partied—a welcome release from their rigorous life.

After 1858 the tide changed. The side-wheel steamer, "*Surprise*", conquered the Fraser to Fort Hope which then became the trade terminal and condemned Fort Langley to a slow death.

In 1956 the Provincial and Federal Governments undertook the partial reconstruction of the Big House, a bastion, the palisades and the *Artisan* building. One original Hudson Bay building remains which served as a warehouse and tradestore, and now houses an intriguing display of goods (*top right*).

The Fort Langley National Historic Park attracts thousands of visitors and is open year round.

Potter's Clydesdales

Bred originally in Scotland, the Clydesdale was used as a work horse in the 1900's.

Potter's Clydesdales of Langley, B.C. are the only Clydesdale team in Canada. The hand-carved 5-ton wagon is drawn by a specially-trained eight-horse team valued at $100,000. Each horse wears a crown symbolizing his Royal Scottish breeding.

Wherever these Clydesdales appear in parades, they bring nostalgia for the good ol' days.

(top) Abbotsford Air Show

92

(lower) Camping at Cultus Lake   (right) Benedictine Abbey overlooking Mission City

After exploring the Fraser Valley our journey comes to an end at the resort of Harrison Hot Springs which nestles by Harrison Lake at the foot of the Coast Mountains.

Surrounding lodges, motels and restaurants in this pretty community are open to tourists mainly from May to September. For year-round activities, The Harrison hotel has a deluxe setting with facilities and sports to suit all seasons.

From this delightful playground, the vastness and splendor of British Columbia's interior beckons to welcome natives and visitors throughout the year.

Contents

Acknowledgements:

The author of the text wishes to acknowledge the assistance of the Vancouver Visitors Bureau, the Vancouver Park Board, Vancouver Public Library, City Archives, Chambers of Commerce for Richmond, Delta, Surrey, Burnaby, New Westminster, North and West Vancouver, Department of Travel Industry— B.C. Information Centre, Vancouver Sun, Vancouver Province, Gastown Guardian, authors Alan Morley, Raymond Hull and Reg Watts, the University of British Columbia, Simon Fraser University, the Burrard Indian Band and many, many others for their invaluable help and interest.

Credits:

Design: Geoffrey Traunter, Copy consultant: Raymond Hull,
Special photographic credits: Potter Distilleries Ltd., pages 90-91,
William Clark: pages 4, 5, 15 (*lower right*), 25 (*lower right*), 26 (*upper*),
40, 41 (*left*), 54 (*upper*), 56 (*left*), 60, 64 (*lower left*), 70 (*left*), 80, 92 (*lower*).
Colour separations: Wy'east Color, Inc., Portland, Ore., U.S.A.
Typesetting: Photype Centre Ltd., Vancouver, B.C., Canada.
Lithography: Agency Press Ltd., Vancouver, B.C., Canada.
'A Toast,' from 'Flint and Feather' by E. Pauline Johnson, courtesy Hodder & Stoughton Limited, Toronto.

About the authors

After five years of travel, Ted Czolowski again focuses his camera on Vancouver.

Czolowski was born and raised in Poland. In 1947, with the Second World War behind him, he made Vancouver his home. As he often says, "I did not adopt the city. The city adopted me, and I am grateful!"

His first "Thank You" to Vancouver was the book, *Through Lions Gate*, published in 1966 by the Greater Vancouver Real Estate Board. This was followed by— *Vancouver Island, Hawaii's Enchanted Islands, Lure of the Carribean, Under All Is The Land, Legacy To Behold* and *Hawaii Calling*. In *Vancouver Calling* he recaptures his beloved city in her different moods.

A former Calgarian, Balynn Richards, moved to New York to study drama. While there she worked in the field of advertising/public relations before going to San Francisco to further her education.

She moved to Vancouver in 1961, instantly felt at home, and has worked in advertising, public relations, and magazine article writing ever since.

In 1971 she wrote the text for *Hawaii Calling*, which became a particular success on the Islands in a Japanese translation.

Now in partnership with Czolowski and artist/designer Geoffrey Traunter, she captures the nostalgia of days past, and the exciting present, in *Vancouver Calling*.